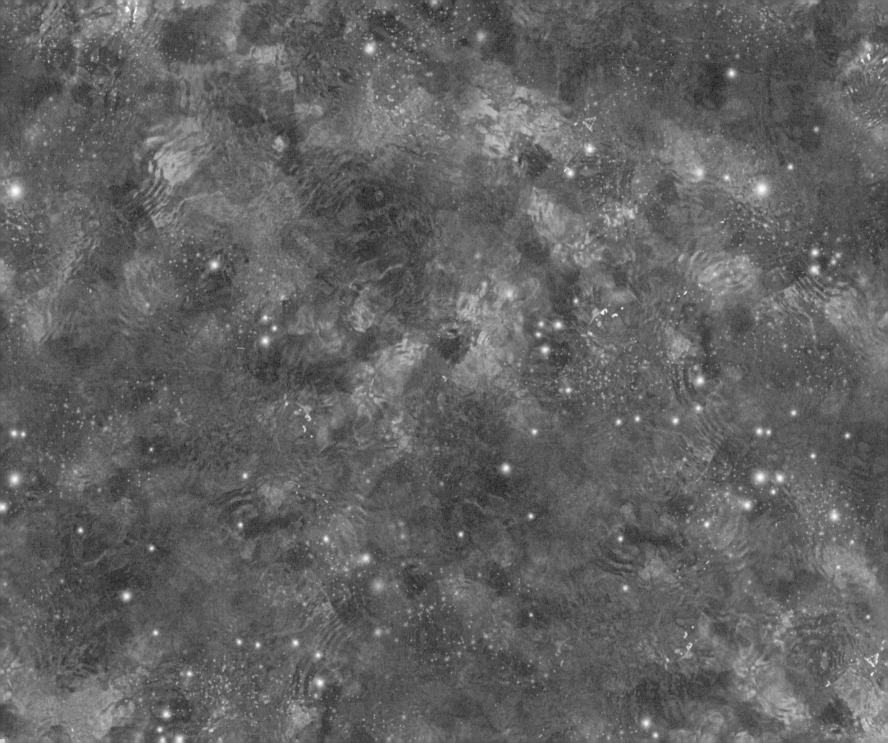

Contents

Contents
continued

HOUGHTON MIFFLIN
Science

Acknowledgements

Literature Selections

Excerpt from *Rocks: Hard, Soft, Smooth, and Rough*, by Natalie M. Rosinsky, illustrated by Matthew John. Copyright © 2003 by Picture Window Books. Reprinted by permission of Picture Window Books.

Excerpt from *We All Go Traveling By*, by Sheena Roberts, illustrated by Siobhan Bell. First published in 2003 by Barefoot Books, Inc. Text copyright © 1995 by Sheena Roberts. Illustrations copyright © 2003 by Siobhan Bell. Reprinted by permission of Barefoot Books, Inc.

Excerpt from *How a Seed Grows*, by Helene J. Jordan, illustrated by Loretta Krupinski. Text copyright © 1960, 1992 by Helene Jordan Waddell. Illustrations copyright © 1992 by Loretta Krupinski. Reprinted by permission of HarperCollins Publishers.

Excerpt from *Each Living Thing*, by Joanne Ryder, illustrated by Ashley Wolff. Text copyright © 2000 by Joanne Ryder. Illustrations copyright © 2000 by Ashley Wolff. Reprinted by permission of Harcourt, Inc. This material may not be reproduced in any form or by any means without the prior written permission of the publisher.

Excerpt from *Sand in My Shoes*, by Wendy Kesselman, illustrated by Ronald Himler. Text copyright © 1995 by Wendy Kesselman. Illustrations copyright © 1995 by Ronald Himler. Reprinted by permission of Hyperion Books for Children.

Excerpt from *It's Spring*, by Linda Glaser, illustrated by Susan Swan. Text copyright © 2002 by Linda Glaser. Illustrations copyright © 2002 by Susan Swan. Used by permission of Millbrook Press, a division of Lerner Publishing Group. All rights reserved.

Excerpt from *What Makes a Shadow?*, by Clyde Robert Bulla, illustrated by June Otani. Text copyright © 1962, 1994 by Clyde Robert Bulla. Illustrations copyright © 1994 by June Otani. Reprinted by permission of HarperCollins Publishers.

Credits

Cover:
©Jeff Hunter/The Image Bank/Getty Images.

Photography:
TOC1 Peter Weber/Photographer's Choice/Getty Images. **TOC2** ©HMCo./Scott Goodwin Photography. **1** ©Myrleen Ferguson Cate/Photo Edit. **3** (bl) Peter Weber/Photographer's Choice/Getty Images. (br) ©Daryl Benson/Masterfile/www.masterfile.com. (tl) ©Anthony Bannister; Gallo Images/CORBIS. (tr) Siede Preis/Getty Images. **5** (bl) Tim Laman/National Geographic/Getty Images. (br) Geoff du Feu/The Image Bank/Getty Images. (c) ©Brandon Cole/www.brandoncole.com. (tl) ©Cisco Castelijns/Foto Natura/Minden Pictures. (tr) ©CHAS. & ELIZABETH SCHWARTZ TRUST/Animals Animals-Earth Scenes. **6** (bl) Art Wolfe/The Image Bank/ Getty Images. (br) Tim Flach/Stone/Getty Images. (c) ©David Boag/Alamy Images. (tl) JH Pete Carmichael/The Image Bank/Getty Images. (tr) ©KENT, BRECK P./Animals Animals-Earth Scenes. **7** (bc) Bill Ling/DK Images. (bl) ©John Daniels/ardea.com. (br) Sharon Eide & Elizabeth Flynn/Sandephoto.com. (tc) klein/Peter Arnold, Inc. (tl) ©BARRY RUNK/STAN/Grant Heilman Photography. (tr) GK Hart/Vikki Hart/Getty Images. **8** (bc) Steve Maslowski/Photo Researchers, Inc. (bc) ©Theo Allofs/Visuals Unlimited. (bl) John Shaw/Burce Coleman, Inc. (br) ©Arthur Morris/CORBIS. (tc) ©Michio Hoshino/Minden Pictures. (tl) Fred Bruemmer/Peter Arnold, Inc. (tr) ©Royalty-Free/CORBIS. **9** ©Phil Degginger/Color-Pic, Inc. **12** (bl) ©David Muench/CORBIS. (br) (cr) ©E.R. Degginger/Color-Pic, Inc. (cl) ©Gilbert S. Grant/Photo Researchers, Inc. (l) ©Raymond Gehman/CORBIS. (r) ©Rich Iwasaki/Stone/Getty Images. (tl) ©Martin B. Withers; Frank Lane Picture Agency/CORBIS. (tr) ©John Kaprielian/Photo Researchers, Inc. **13** (bl) ©Theo Allofs/Visuals Unlimited. (bl) Steve Maslowski/Photo Researchers, Inc. (br) Gilbert S. Grant/Photo Researchers, Inc. (c) Phil Degginger/Color-Pic, Inc. (c) klein/Peter Arnold, Inc. (tl) Geoff du Feu/The Image Bank/Getty Images. (tr) ©E.R. Degginger/Color-Pic, Inc. **14** ©Martin Rugner/AGE Fotostock America. **17** (bl) ©Gil Lopez-Espina/Visuals Unlimited. (br) ©ROTENBERG, NANCY/Animals Animals-Earth Scenes. (c) ©Rudi Von Briel/Photo Edit. (tl) ©Simon Bruty/Stone/Getty Images. (tr) ©SHRIK DAVID L./Animals Animals-Earth Scenes. **18** (bl) ©Fritz Polking/Visuals Unlimited. (br) ©Studio Carlo Dani/Animals Animals-Earth Scenes. (cl) ©Gary Bumgarner/Photographer's Choice/Getty Images. (cr) ©LACZ, GERARD/Animals Animals-Earth Scenes. (tl) (tr) Scott Camazine/Photo Researchers, Inc. **19** (bl) ©Kim Fennema/Visuals Unlimited. (br) ©Suzanne L. & Joseph T. Collins/Photo Researchers, Inc. (c) ©Larry Miller/Photo Researchers, Inc. (tr) ©Gary Meszaros/Visuals Unlimited. **20** (bl) ©Edward Kinsman/Photo Researchers, Inc. (br) ©LACZ, GERARD/Animals Animals-Earth Scenes. (c) ©Adrian Davies/Nature Picture Library. (tl) ©Dennis Drenner/Visuals Unlimited. **21** ©Deborah L. Barker. **22** (br) ©Asgeir Helgestad/Nature Picture Library. (c) ©PONTIER, JOHN/Animals Animals-Earth Scenes. (tr) ©Gary Meszaros/Visuals Unlimited. (tr) ©Rod Planck/Photo Researchers, Inc. **23** (br) Colin Preston/Nature Picture Library. (c) ©Wild & Natural/Animals Animals-Earth Scenes. (tl) ©Valan Photos. (tr) ©Charles Sleicher/Stone/Getty Images. **24** (bl) ©Larry Miller/Photo Researchers, Inc. (br) ©Colin Preston/Nature Picture Library. (tr) ©Gil Lopez-Espina/Visuals Unlimited. **25** Kevin Anthony Horgan/The Image Bank/Getty Images. **27** (c) ©Digital Vision/Getty Images. (l) ©Michele Westmorland/CORBIS. (r) Peter Griffith/Masterfile.com. **28** (bl) ©David Wrench/LGPL/Alamy Images. (c) ©LARRY LEFEVER/Grant Heilman Photography. (tr) ©Daryl Benson/Masterfile/www.masterfile.com. **29** (bl) ©Andre Jenny/Alamy Images. (c) ©Bill Brooks/Alamy Images. (tr) ©Royalty-Free/CORBIS. **31** (c) ©Ron Watts/CORBIS. (r) ©Adam Jones/Visuals Unlimited. **33** (bl) ©Bill Brooks/Alamy Images. (c) ©Ron Watts/CORBIS. (tl) ©Daryl Benson/Masterfile/www.masterfile.com. **34** Ryan McVay/Photodisc Red/Getty Images. **36** (bc) (bkgd) ©Tom McCarthy/Photo Edit. (br) ©Mary McCulley/ImageState. (cl) ©Nancy Sheehan/Photo Edit. (tr) Shaun Egan/Photographer's Choice/Getty Images. **37** (bc) ©Boden/Ledingham/Masterfile/www.masterfile.com. (c) ©Richard Hutchings/Photo Edit. **38** (c) CORBIS/Creatas Stock Resources. (l) ©Joe Swift/Index Stock Imagery. (r) ©Alamy Images. **39** (c) ©Myrleen Ferguson Cate/Photo Edit. (l) ©Bluestone Productions/SuperStock. (r) ©Tom Stewart/CORBIS. **40** (c) ©Bill Frymire/Masterfile/www.masterfile.com. (l) Sarah M. Golonka/FoodPix/Getty Images. (r) Don Smetzer/Stone/Getty Images. **42** (c) Photodisc Collection/Photodisc Blue/Getty Images. (l) Anne Ackerman/Taxi/Getty Images. (r) SW Productions/Brand X Pictures/Getty Images. **43** (bc) ©Bill Aron/Photo Edit. (bl) ©Chad Slattery/Stone/Getty Images. (br) ©Myrleen Ferguson Cate/Photo Edit. (cl) ©Bill Frymire/Masterfile/www.masterfile.com. (l) ©Tom McCarthy/Photo Edit. (tc) ©Richard Hutchings/Photo Edit. (tc) ©Alamy Images. **45** Adrian Myers/Photographer's Choice/Getty Images. **47** (bl) ©Behling & Johnson. **50** ©DK Images. **51** (c) ©Comstock IMAGES. (l) ©Index Stock/Alamy Images. (r) Ryan McVay/Photodisc Green/Getty Images. **54** (bl) ©DK Images. **55** ©Rommel/Masterfile/www.masterfile.com. **57** (c) ©Peter M. Fisher/CORBIS. (l) ©Alan Oddie/Photo Edit. (r) Bryan Mullennix/Photodisc Red/Getty Images. **58** (bl) ©David Young-Wolf/Photo Edit. (br) ©Susan Van Etten/Photo Edit. (c) ©Age Fotostock/SuperStock. (tl) ©Lester Lefkowitz/CORBIS. **61** (bl) ©NOVASTOCK/Photo Edit. (br) ©Merritt Vincent/Photo Edit. (c) ©Stewart Cohen/Stone/Getty Images. (tl) ©D. Hurst/Almay Images. (tr) ©David Martyn Hughes/Alamy Images. **62** (bl) ©Brad Wilson/Photonica. (br) ©Duomo/CORBIS. (c) ©Eric Fowke/Photo Edit. (tl) ©Ariel Skelley/CORBIS. (tr) ©Jack Hollingsworth/CORBIS. **63** (bl) Comstock Images/Alamy Images. (c) ©Image Source/Alamy Images. (tr) ©Ariel Skelley/CORBIS. **64** (bkgd) ©Peter Griffith/Masterfile/www.masterfile.com. (c) Cheri Lord/The Ottumwa Courier/AP Wide World Photos. (l) Amy Sancetta/AP Wide World Photos. (r) ©Theo Allofs/CORBIS. **65** (c) ©D. Hurst/Alamy Images. (r) Amy Sancetta/AP Wide World Photos. (tl) Bryan Mullennix/Photodisc Red/Getty Images.

Assignment:
Wheelchairs provided courtesy of Colours in Motion. **4** ©HMCo./Angela Coppola Photography. **27** (bc) (bl) (br) ©HMCo./Angela Coppola Photography. **32** ©HMCo./Angela Coppola Photography. **33** (r) ©HMCo./Angela Coppola Photography. **37** (tr) ©HMCo./Sonny Senser/sonnyphoto.com. **47** (br) (c) (cr) (tl) ©HMCo./Angela Coppola Photography. (tr) ©HMCo./Joel Benjamin Photography. **48** ©HMCo./Scott Goodwin Photography. **49** ©HMCo./Scott Goodwin Photography. **52** ©HMCo./Angela Coppola Photography. **53** ©HMCo./Angela Coppola Photography. **54** (r) ©HMCo./Angela Coppola Photography. (tl) (tr) ©HMCo./Scott Goodwin Photography. **58** (tr) ©HMCo./Scott Goodwin Photography. **61** (tr) ©HMCo./Bruton Stroube. **65** (tc) ©HMCo./Scott Goodwin Photography.

Illustration:
10 Patrica Rossi Calkin. **11** Patrica Rossi Calkin. **16** Dave Klug. **19** (c) Luigi Galante. **20** (c) Luigi Galante. **22** (c) Tom Leonard. **23** (c) Tom Leonard. **41** Mircea Catusanu. **43** (c) (f) (r) Chris Vallo. **59** Mircea Catusanu. **60** Mircea Catusanu. **65** (bl) Mircea Catusanu.

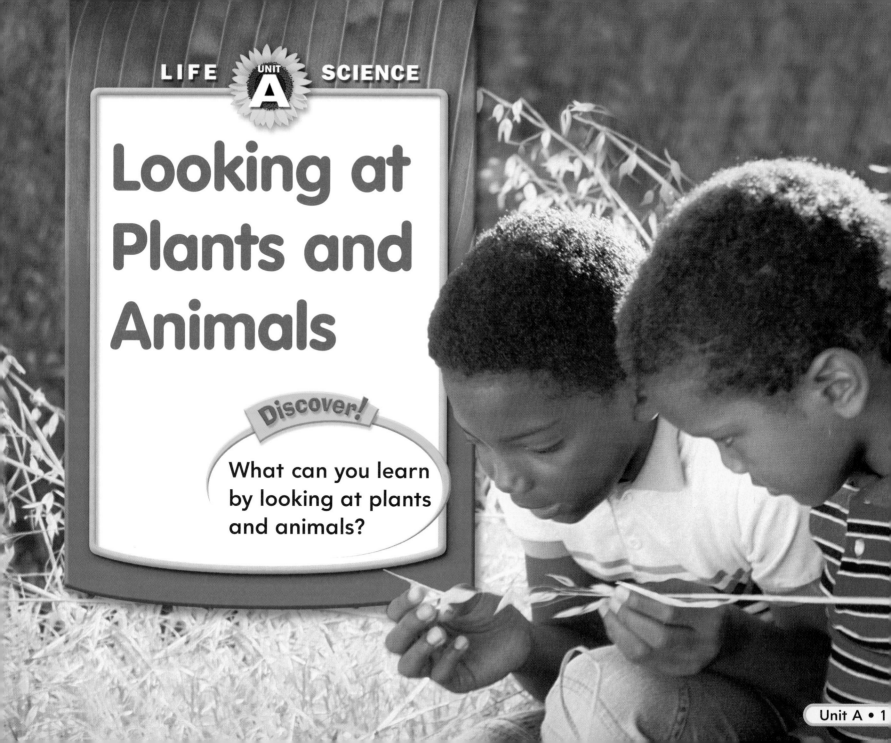

LIFE **UNIT A** SCIENCE

Looking at Plants and Animals

Discover!

What can you learn by looking at plants and animals?

How a Seed Grows
by Helene J. Jordan

A seed needs many things to grow.

It needs soil

and water

and sun.

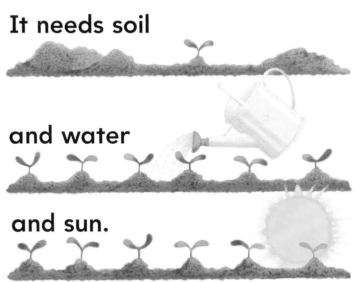

UNIT A What does a seed need to grow?

Animal Body Parts

Animals have different **body parts**.

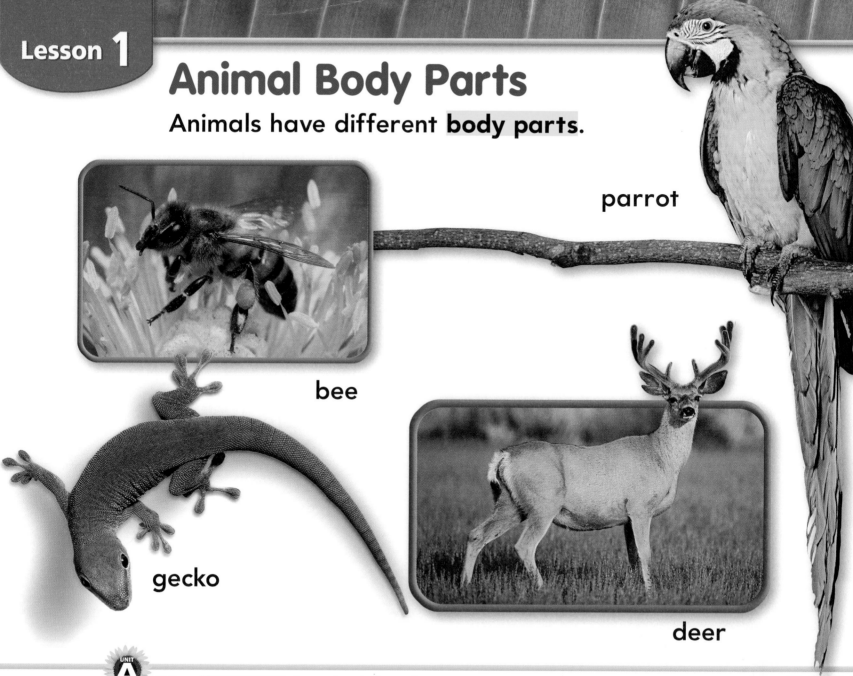

parrot

bee

gecko

deer

What **body parts** do animals have?

Your Body Parts

People have parts, too. Your body parts help you bend and move.

head

nose

elbow

eyes

hand

ears

trunk

mouth

arm

knee

leg

foot

How do you use your body parts?

Animals That Swim and Fly

Some animals use their parts to swim and fly.

 How do **fins**, **wings**, and **tails** help animals swim or fly?

Unit A • 5

Animals That Walk, Hop, and Crawl

These animals move in different ways.

Growing Animals

An **adult** animal has **offspring**, or young. The offspring grow.

A

How can you tell which **adult** and **offspring** go together?

Unit A • 7

Sort Birds

You can **sort**, or group, animals.
Group these birds by body part or color.

How did you **sort** the birds?

Plant Parts

flower

leaf

roots

stem

Plants Grow and Change

Many plants grow from **seeds**.

❶ Seeds **sprout** and grow.

❷ First, the root grows.

❸ The stem grows.

❹ Leaves form.

 How does a **seed** change as it grows?

Plants Grow and Change

5 The plant keeps growing.

6 Flowers form. **Flowers** make fruit.

7 **Seeds** form in the **fruit**.

8 New plants can grow from the seeds.

 Where do **seeds** form?

Compare Trees

The stem of a tree is called a **trunk**.

needles

cones

bark

pine tree

leaves

seeds

bark

maple tree

 How are these trees the same and different?

Talk About Plants and Animals

How does this duck move?

How will the piglet change?

How are these birds different?

What are the parts of this plant?

How can you compare plants?

 Discover!

What can you learn by looking at plants and animals?

Where Plants and Animals Live

Discover!

Where can you find plants and animals?

Each Living Thing

by Joanne Ryder

Watch out for every living thing,
for all beasts fine and free,
who grace the earth
and ride the skies
and glide within the sea.

Living and Nonliving Things

Living things grow and change. **Nonliving things** do not grow and change.

Needs of Living Things

All living things need food, air, and water.
Animals need **shelter**, or a place to live.
Plants need sunlight and space.

air

water

food

shelter

space

B What do living things need?

What Animals Eat

Food gives animals energy.
Different animals eat different things.

Meat Eaters

Plant Eaters

What do animals eat?

Pond Life

Many plants and animals live in or near the **pond.**

What plants and animals can you find?

Hidden Pond Life

Look closely. You can see even more living things near the **pond**.

What other living things can you find?

Deb Barker, Wildlife Photographer

Deb Barker takes pictures of plants and animals where they live. Her pictures help people learn about living things.

UNIT B What can you learn by looking at wildlife photographs?

Unit B • 21

Meadow Life

A grassy area called
a **meadow** is near the pond.
Plants and animals live in the meadow.

Hidden Meadow Life

Look closely. You can see even more living things in the **meadow**.

Talk About Living Things

Lesson 1

What living and nonliving things can you name?

Lessons 2 3

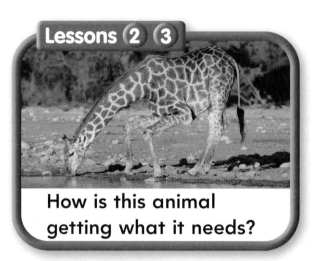

How is this animal getting what it needs?

Lesson 4

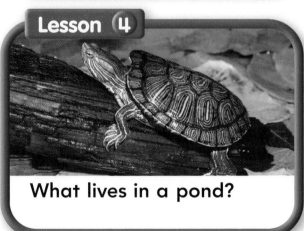

What lives in a pond?

Lesson 5

What lives in a meadow?

Discover!

Where can you find plants and animals?

Looking at Earth

Discover!

What materials make up our Earth?

Rocks: Hard, Soft, Smooth, and Rough

By Natalie M. Rosinsky

See the rock at your feet? Pick it up.
Is it smooth and sparkly? Is it soft and sandy?
Is it marked with the shape of a shell?

How are rocks different?

Earth's Materials

Earth's **materials** are land, water, and air.

Land	Water	Air

Land is the part of Earth you live on.

All living things need water.

You breathe air. Air is all around you.

Where can you find air?

Earth's Land

Land is the part of Earth that we live on. It can be rough or flat. It can be high or low.

mountains

plain

valley

On what part of Earth do we live?

Earth's Water

Water in the **ocean** is salty.
Water in most rivers and
lakes is fresh.

lake

ocean

river

Where can you find Earth's water?

Sand in My Shoes

By Wendy Kesselman

One last look, one last touch
One last climb up the dune
How can the summer be over so soon?

Changing Land

Water changes land.

Wind changes land.

How does land **change**?

Saving Earth's Materials

Earth's materials can be used up.
You can help **save** Earth's materials.

Save water.

Save energy.

UNIT C

How can you help **save** Earth's materials?

Unit C • 32

Talk About Earth

Lessons ① ②

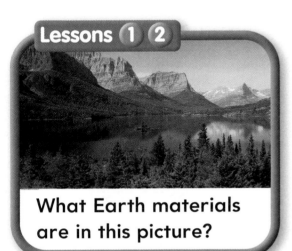

What Earth materials are in this picture?

Lesson ③

What kind of water is in the ocean?

Lesson ④

What happened to the land here?

Lesson ⑤

How is this child caring for Earth?

Discover!

What materials make up our Earth?

Looking at the Sky

Discover!

What can you tell from looking at the sky?

It's Spring!
By Linda Glaser

The ground is growing
soft and warm again.
There's a clean fresh
smell in the air.
We find tiny new green
growing things everywhere.
Animals that slept all winter
are now waking up—
earthworms, frogs, turtles,
snakes, beetles, ladybugs.

UNIT D How can you tell that it is spring?

Kinds of Weather

Weather is what it is like outside.
Temperature, wind, and the sky tell about weather.

Cold

Windy

Rainy

Sunny and Hot

What clues tell about the **weather**?

Winter Weather

Winter is the coldest season of the year.

In some places, winter is cool but not cold.

In winter, people wear clothes that help them keep warm.

Days are shorter in winter

What clues tell you that it is **winter**?

Spring Weather

In **spring**, the weather warms.

Farmers plant crops.

Rain falls.
Flowers bloom.

Wind blows.

What clues tell you that it is **spring**?

Summer Weather

Summer is the hottest season of the year.

People keep cool.

Plants grow.

Ice cream will melt.

UNIT D What clues tell you that it is **summer**?

Fall Weather

Days become shorter and cooler during **fall**.

Crops are picked.

Leaves change color.

In some places, the weather stays warm.

What clues tell you that it is **fall**?

Day and Night

Day

Night

How are the pictures the same and different?

Day and Night Activities

Make time for healthful activities every day.

Eat healthful foods.

Be active.

Get plenty of sleep.

How do you keep your body healthy?

The Sun in the Sky

Sunrise	Noon	Sunset

How does the **Sun** seem to move across the sky?

Talk About Weather and Seasons

Lesson ①

What clues tell you about the weather?

Lessons ② ③

How does weather change from winter to spring?

Lessons ④ ⑤

How does what you wear change with the season?

Lessons ⑥ ⑦

How is the night sky different from the day sky?

Discover!

What can you tell from looking at the sky?

Observing Objects

Discover!

How can you tell one object from another?

We All Go Traveling By

By Sheena Roberts

I spy with my little eye,
You can hear with your little ear,
A long blue train goes chuff-chuff-chuff.

A bright red truck goes rumble-rumble-rumble.
A yellow school bus goes beep-beep-beep.

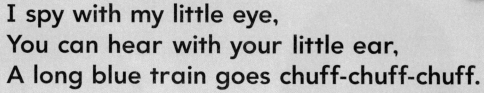

How are the people traveling in this picture?

Your Senses

You have five **senses**.

seeing

hearing

smelling

touching

tasting

What **senses** do you have?

Sort Objects

You can sort **objects** in many ways.

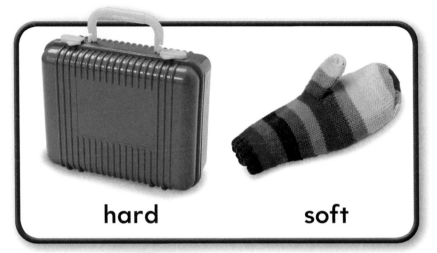

hard   soft

rough   smooth

big   little

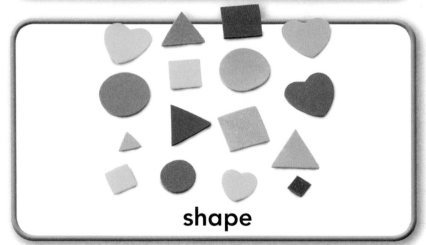

shape

UNIT E

How can you sort **objects**?

Make Changes

You can change objects.

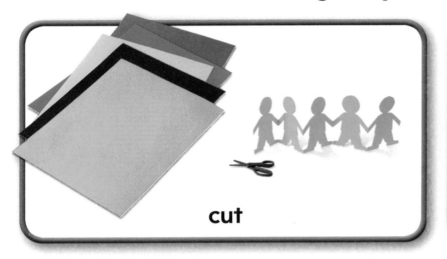

cut

mix

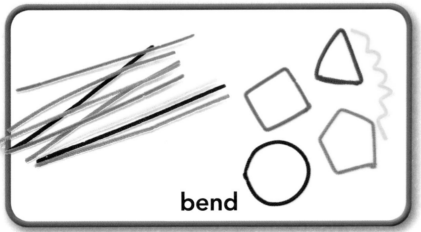

bend

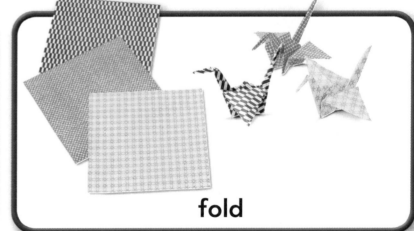

fold

How can you change objects?

Different Materials

Some things are made of many different **materials**.

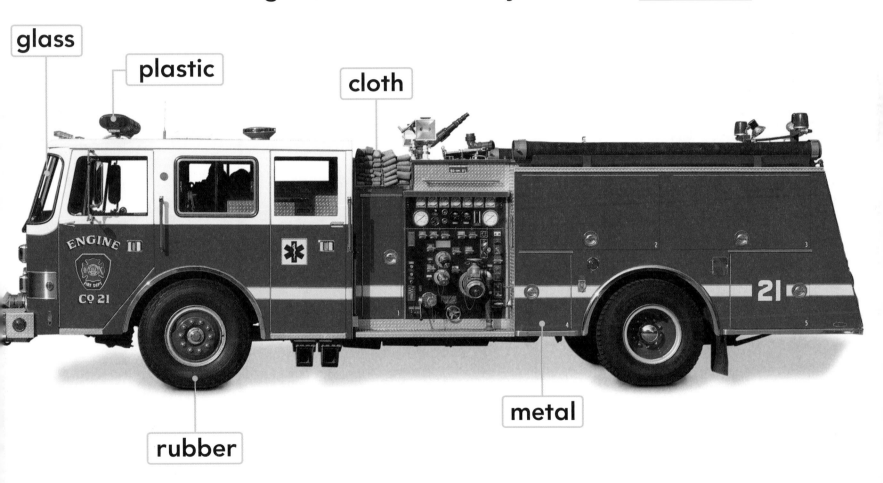

glass

plastic

cloth

rubber

metal

What **materials** make up the truck?

Technology

Telephones Then and Now

100 years ago

50 years ago

Today

How have telephones changed over time?

Parts Work Together

Most things are made of many **parts**. The parts work together.

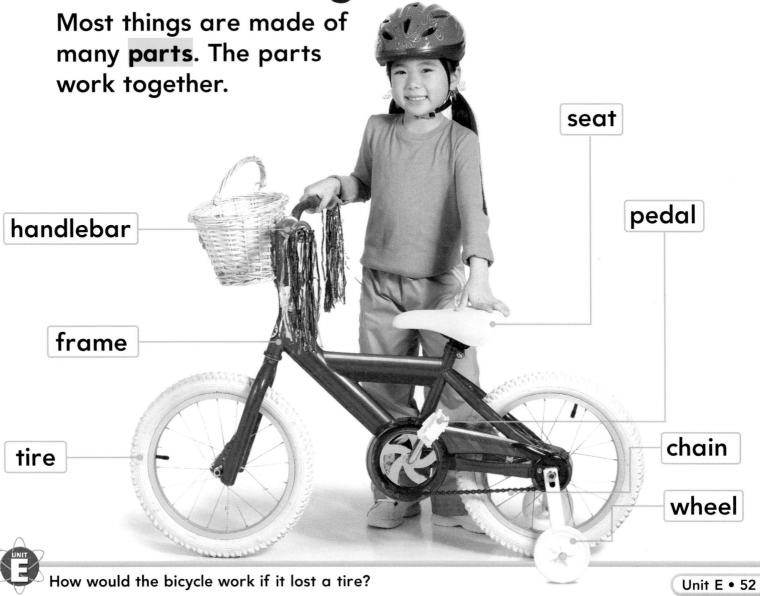

seat

pedal

handlebar

frame

tire

chain

wheel

How would the bicycle work if it lost a tire?

Solids, Liquids, and Gases

Solid

Liquid

Gas

 What **solids**, **liquids**, and **gases** can you name?

Talk About Objects

Lessons 1 2

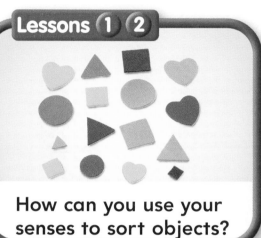

How can you use your senses to sort objects?

Lesson 3

How has the paper been changed?

Lesson 6

Is water a solid, a liquid, or a gas?

Lessons 4 5

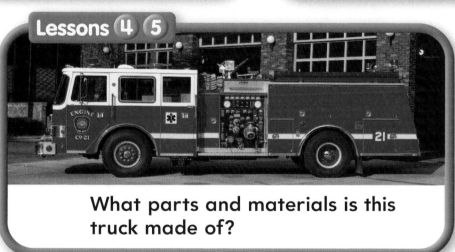

What parts and materials is this truck made of?

Discover!

How can you tell one object from another?

Things That Move

Discover!

How can you change how things move?

What Makes a Shadow?

by Clyde Robert Bulla

When the sun is in front of you, look behind you. You can see your shadow. When you move, your shadow moves. When you run, your shadow runs. But you can never catch it.

Where is your shadow when the Sun is in front of you?

Finding Shadows

Solid objects block the light.
They make a shadow.

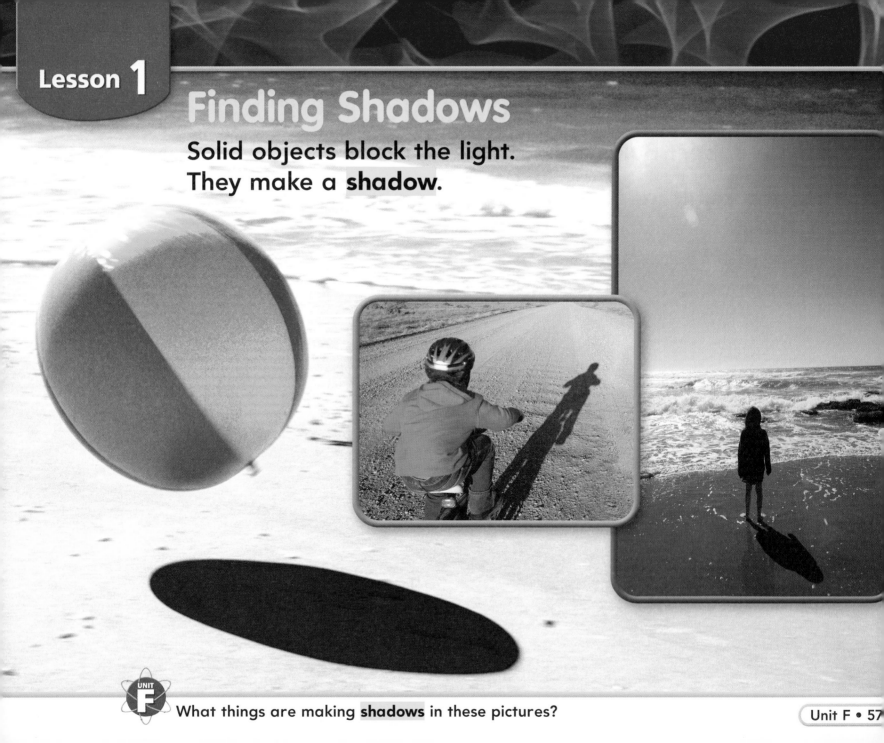

What things are making **shadows** in these pictures?

Things That Make Heat

Things that are warm give off **heat**.

Sun

burning candles

electrical things

stove

fire

City Sounds

Many things make **sound** in the city.

What **sounds** might you hear in the city?

Country Sounds

Many things make **sound** in the country.

What **sounds** might you hear in the country?

How Things Move

Objects **move** in different ways.

spin

zigzag

back and forth

up and down

straight

UNIT **F**
How do these objects **move**?

Focus On

Health and Safety

Play Safely

Pushes and Pulls

A **push** moves something away from you.
A **pull** moves something closer to you.

How do these things move when they are pushed or pulled?

Up and Down

 What happens when things go up?

Talk About How Things Move

Lesson 1

How is a shadow made?

Lesson 2
What is giving off heat in this picture?

Lesson 3
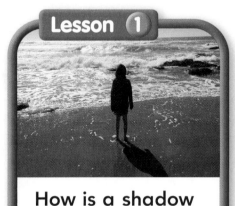
What sounds might you hear in a city?

Lessons 4 5

How is this top moving?

Lesson 6

What happens when things go up in the air?

Discover!

How can you change how things move?